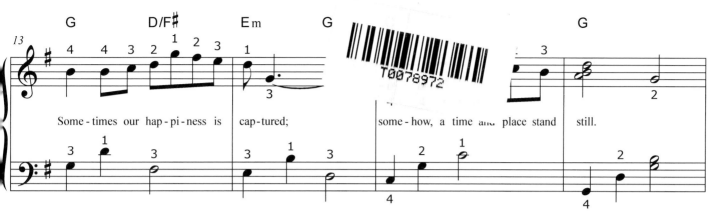

Some - times our hap - pi - ness is cap - tured; some - how, a time and place stand still.

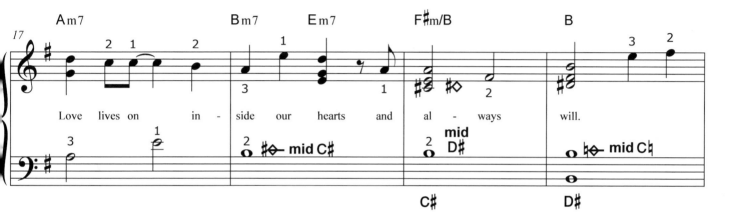

Love lives on in - side our hearts and al - ways will.

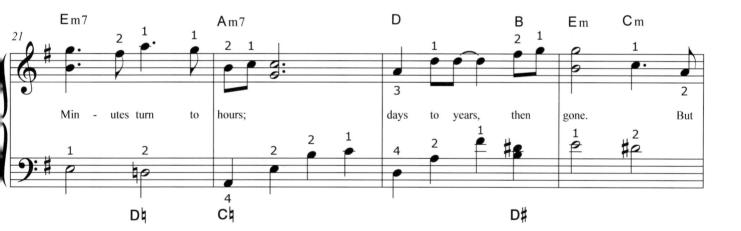

Min - utes turn to hours; days to years, then gone. But

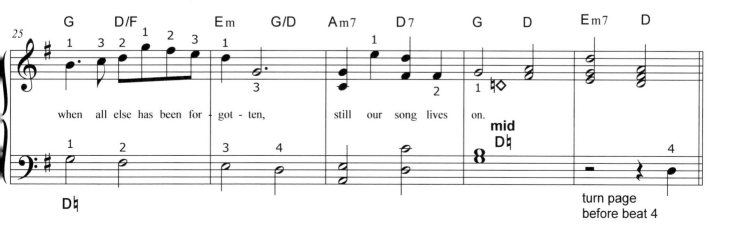

when all else has been for - got - ten, still our song lives on.

turn page
before beat 4

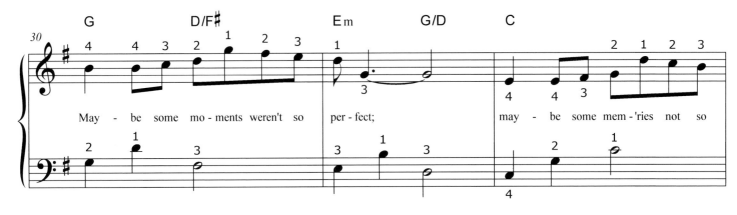

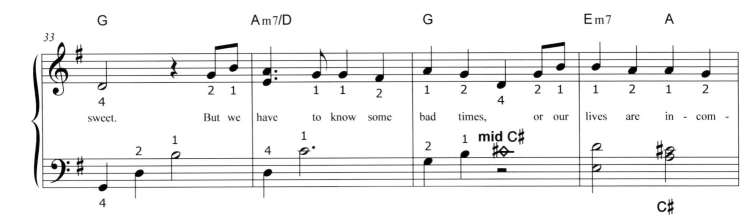

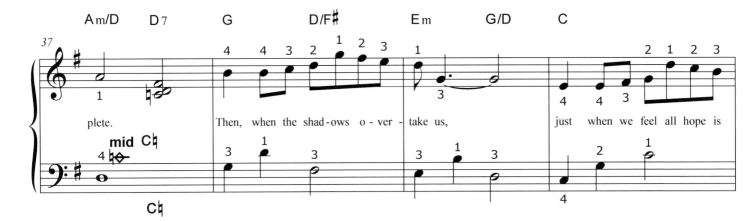

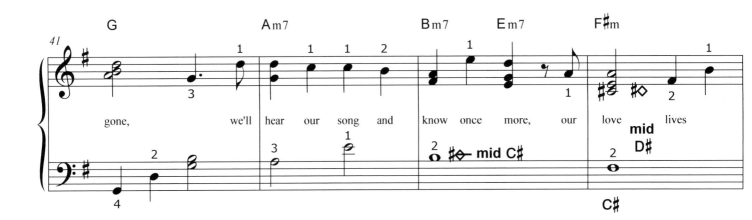

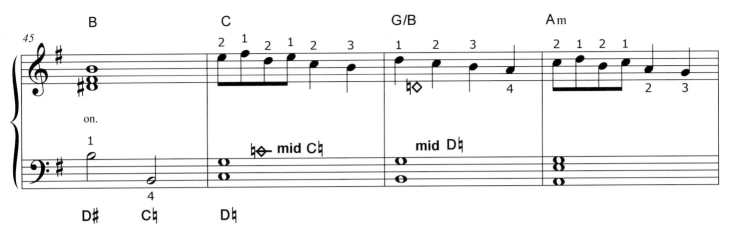

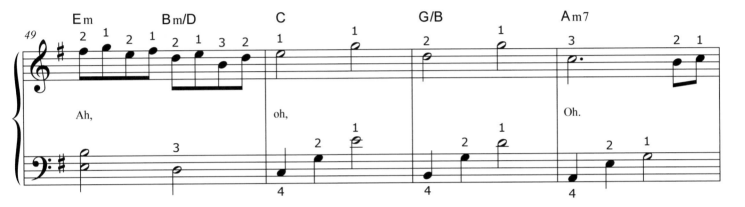

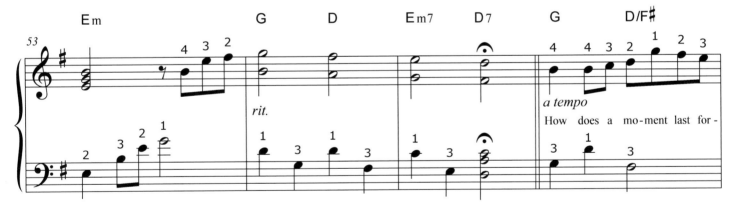

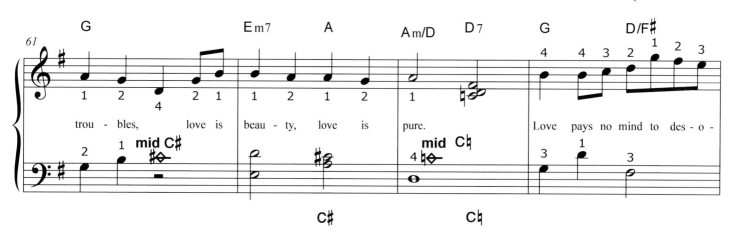

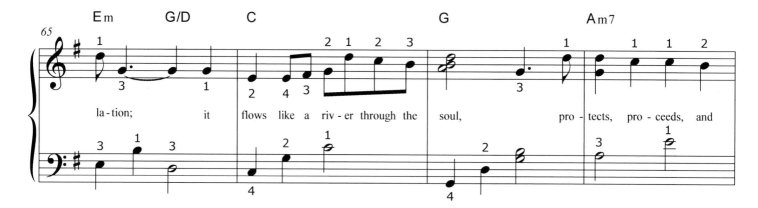

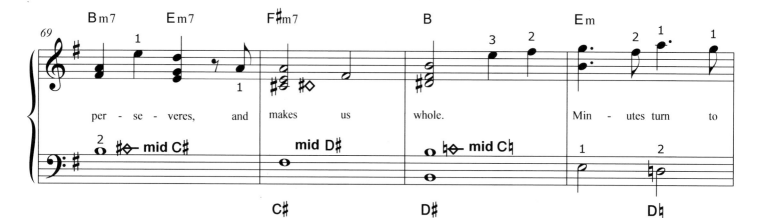

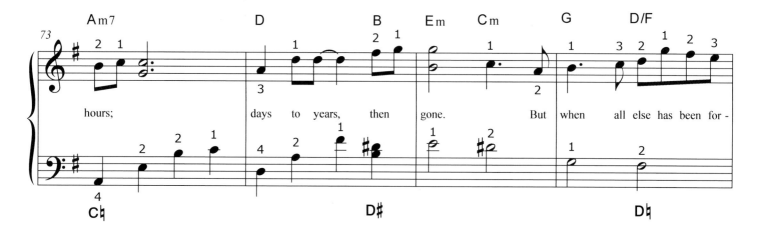